Copyright: 2022 Tamela Rowe

Layout and typesetting: Hatice Bayramoglu

All rights reserved. No part of this book may be reproduced, stored in a retrieval system, or transmitted by any means, electronic, mechanical, photocopying, recording or otherwise, without the express written permission of the copyright holders.

Lexi Renee

A day at the Park

Lexi Renee

Lexi woke up bright and early, wagging her tail ready to play. Today she was going to the dog park.

Lexi
Renee

Lexi was so excited!
She hurried to eat her breakfast.
Before she went to the dog park.

7

After Lexi finished eating she went to Cam's room. Cam is Lexi's human brother. Cam would walk and feed Lexi every day. Lexi loved to hide Cams slippers and chase him around the house.

" Ruff, ruff!" Lexi barked. "Not now Lexi ". Cam said with his eyes still closed.

Lexi went to Taja's room next. Taja is her human sister. She would sneak treats to Lexi and comb her fur with a sparkling hot pink brush. Lexi loved giving Taja kisses." Ruff, ruff!" Lexi barked. Taja pulled the covers from her head, "Later Lexi". She said.

Lexi was so sad. She went back to her room and looked out the window. Lexi saw other dogs playing. She made a sad puppy dog face.

Suddenly it started to rain. This is the worst day ever, Lexi thought to herself.

Lexi was sad, but she was not mad. She dediced to go lay next to Cam to take a nap. A few minutes later she was fast asleep.

When Lexi woke from her nap, Cam was up, dressed,and ready to go. Lexi remembered it had rained, she ran to the window to look outside. There was a big, beautiful rainbow and the other neighborhood dogs were back outside playing.

Taja walked in the room holding Lexi's favorite sparkling leash.''Hey Lexi. Ready to go outside?'' She asked.
''Ruff,ruff''
Lexi barked happily. They were finally ready to head to the park.

When Lexi got to the dog park two of her favorite friends were already there.
''Ruff,ruff, ruff, ruff, ruff!'' Lexi barked with excitment.
She had so much fun running around and playing all day.

Taja + Lexi + Cam
Park Day!

Lexi was so happy she licked Cam and Taja's face.
Lexi was never mad when things did not go her way,
she tried her best to be patient and understanding,
and because of that Lexi had the best day ever!

www.ingramcontent.com/pod-product-compliance
Lightning Source LLC
LaVergne TN
LVHW071234160826
845679LV00003B/987
9798849538020